▤ Collins Educational

Dear Colleague

Collins Primary Geography

Thank you for requesting World Watch Teacher's Guide 1. This book, and its accompanying pupil book, are the first in a four-stage geography series for pupils aged 7-11. World Watch 2 will be published in September 1994, and books 3 and 4 in 1995.

World Watch is an accessible, balanced and well-structured programme which takes into account the time constraints of a foundation subject.

This brochure shows the links between World Watch 1 and the existing geography curriculum which is in force until September 1995. As soon as the statutory orders for the new national curriculum are published (January 1995), we will produce similar detailed links between them and World Watch. These will be available FREE to anyone requesting them. Please complete the form below if you would like to register for them now.

Yours faithfully

Anne Galloway

Anne Galloway
Commissioning Editor

COLLINS PRIMARY GEOGRAPHY

Please complete a photocopy of this form and return it to Collins Educational, Harper Collins Publishers, FREEPOST GW 5078, Bishopbriggs, Glasgow G64 1BR. Fax: 041 306 3750. Or phone 041 306 3269.

_____ Please send me the free brochure linking World Watch 1 with the new 1995 national curriculum as soon as it is available.

Mrs/Ms/Miss/Mr .... Position ....

School ....

Address ....

.... Postcode ....

1991 National Curriculum links

World Watch Books 1 and 2 cover Levels 2-4 of the 1991 national curriculum.

The table below shows how *World Watch* Book 1 covers the geography statements of attainment for England and Wales at Levels 2 and 3. There will also be opportunities for extending the work into Level 4, particularly when using the research pages in the middle of each unit.

Unit	Page	Statements of Attainment
Planet Earth	3	Gg1 3d) Identify features on aerial photographs.
	4-5	Gg2 2c) Identify features of a locality outside the local area and suggest how these might affect the lives of people who live there.
	6	Gg2 3a) Name the features marked on Maps A and C at the end of the programmes of study.
	7	Gg3 3c) Identify and describe a familiar landscape feature.
A Wet Planet	8-9	Gg3 2b) Identify forms in which water occurs in the environment.
	10-11	Gg1 2e) Identify familiar features on photographs and pictures.
	12	Gg1 3a) Use letter/number co-ordinates to locate features on a map.
	13	Gg3 3b) Describe what happens to rainwater when it reaches the ground.
Hot and Cold Places	14-15	Gg3 3a) Describe contrasting weather conditions in parts of the world.
	16	Gg1 2e) Identify familiar features on photographs and pictures.
	17	Gg2 2c) Identify features of a locality outside the local area and suggest how these might affect the lives of people who live there.
	18-19	Gg1 2d) Record weather observations made over a short period. Gg3 2a) Recognise seasonal weather patterns.
A Place to Live	20-21	Gg4 3d) Distinguish between those uses of land which require large sites and those which occupy small sites.
	22-23	Gg4 3b) Identify features of settlements which reveal their functions or origins.
	24-25	Gg2 2b) Describe uses of land and buildings in the local area. Gg4 2a) Demonstrate an understanding that most homes are part of a settlement, and that settlements vary in size.
Ways of Travelling	26-27	Gg4 3c) Explain why different forms of transport are used.
	28	Gg4 2b) Give reasons why people make journeys of different lengths.
	29	Gg4 2d) Identify how goods and services needed in the local community are provided.
	30	Gg1 3b) Use a large-scale map to locate their own position and features outside the classroom.
	31	Gg2 3c) Use correct geographical vocabulary to identify types of landscape features and activities with which they are familiar in the local area.

Unit	Page	Statements of Attainment
Food and Farming	32-33	Gg4 3d) Distinguish between those uses of land which require large sites and those which occupy small sites.
	34-35	Gg4 2c) Identify how goods and services needed in the local community are provided.
	36-37	Gg2 3e) Explain the relationships between types of land-use, buildings and human activity in the local area. Gg2 3f) Explain why some activities in the local area are located where they are.
Caring for the Countryside	38-39	Gg5 2b) Describe ways in which people have changed the environment.
	40-41	Gg2 3a) Name the features marked on Maps A and C at the end of the programmes of study.
	42	Gg5 3b) Describe an activity designed to improve the local environment or a place they have visited.
	43	Gg5 2c) Suggest how they could improve the quality of their own environment.
Scotland	44-45	Gg2 2a) Name the countries of the United Kingdom.
	46-47	Gg2 2d) Describe similarities and differences between the local area and another locality specified in the programme of study. Gg1 2c) Follow a route using a plan. Gg1 3c) Make a map of a short route, showing features in the correct order.
	48-49	Gg2 3d) Compare features and occupations of the local area with the other localities specified in the programme of study. Gg4 3a) Give reasons why people change their homes.
France	50-51	Gg1 2b) Make a representation of a real or imaginary place.
	52-53	Gg1 2a) Use geographical vocabulary to talk about places.
	54-55	Gg1 2e) Identify familiar features on photographs and pictures. Gg2 2c) Identify features of a locality outside the local area and suggest how these might affect the lives of the people who live there.
Asia	56-57	Gg2 3a) Name the features marked on Maps A and C at the end of the programmes of study.
	58	Gg1 2a) Use geographical vocabulary to talk about places.
	59-61	Gg1 2d) Describe similarities and differences between the local area and another locality specified in the programme of study. Gg2 3d) Compare features and occupations in the local area with the other localities specified in the programmes of study.

Copymaster matrix

Theme	Copymaster	National Curriculum link
Landscape	1 Planet Earth	Gg3 3c
	2 Planet Earth	Gg2 2c
Water	3 A Wet Planet	Gg3 2b
	4 A Wet Planet	Gg3 3b
Weather	5 Hot and Cold Places	Gg3 3a
	6 Hot and Cold Places	Gg1 2e
Settlement	7 A Place to Live	Gg4 2a
	8 A Place to Live	Gg1 2b
Transport	9 Ways of Travelling	Gg4 3c
	10 Ways of Travelling	Gg4 2c
Work	11 Food and Farming	Gg3 2a
	12 Food and Farming	Gg4 2c
Environment	13 Caring for the Countryside	Gg5 2b
	14 Caring for the Countryside	Gg5 2c
United Kingdom	15 Scotland	Gg2 2d
	16 Scotland	Gg2 2c
Europe	17 France	Gg1 2a
	18 France	Gg2 3d
World	19 Asia	Gg1 2b
	20 Asia	Gg2 3d

World Watch 1
Teacher's Guide

Contents

Geography in the primary school	2
Collins Primary Geography	3
Structure of the books	4
Using the books	6
Layout of the units	8
Differentiation	10
Assessment	11
Studying the local area	12
Studying contrasting and distant localities	13
Information on the units	14
Copymaster matrix	24
Copymasters	26
Links to the Scottish Guidelines 5-14	46
Links to the Northern Ireland Curriculum	47

Geography in the primary school

Geography is the study of the earth's surface. It helps children understand the human and physical forces which shape the environment. Children are naturally interested in their immediate surroundings. They also want to know about places beyond their direct experience. Geography is uniquely placed to satisfy this curiosity.

Aims of geographical education

Geographical education should:

(a) stimulate pupils' interest in their surroundings and in the variety of physical and human conditions on the Earth's surface

(b) foster their sense of wonder at the beauty of the world around them

(c) help them to develop an informed concern about the quality of the environment and the future of the human habitat, and,

(d) thereby enhance their sense of responsibility for the care of the Earth and its peoples.

Key Stage 1 : P1-3

At Key Stage 1:P1-3 children should be introduced to maps and plans and be encouraged to use and develop geographical vocabulary. They need to find out about their own area, other places in the United Kingdom and the wider world. Themes and cross-curricular topics provide a valuable approach. Pictures, stories and photographs are useful sources of information.

Key Stage 2 : P4-7

At Key Stage 2:P4-7 children should become more proficient at using and handling maps. Place studies should be selected from the local area, other parts of the United Kingdom, mainland Europe and economically developing countries in order to create a broad and balanced curriculum. There will be increasing opportunities for teaching geography either as a subject on its own or as the central component of a wider topic. Children should begin to understand the interaction between people and their physical surroundings. They will also be able to assess environmental issues with a greater degree of sophistication.

Investigations

Throughout the primary school, enquiry and investigation should form an important part of pupils' work. Children should be given opportunities to undertake practical work in the classroom, school building and local environment. By asking questions and searching for answers children will develop the essential knowledge, understanding and skills which form the basis of geography.

Collins Primary Geography

World Watch is a complete geography scheme for children in the primary school. It consists of a photographic *Themes Pack* for infants which overlaps with a set of pupil books (*World Watch* Books 1-4) for juniors. This means that *World Watch* can be used as a structure for teaching geography throughout the primary school from ages 5-11.

World Watch Books 1-4

This graded geography series is designed for children at Key Stage 2:P4-7. There are four books in the series, one for each of the junior years. Each book has an overall focus:

Book 1 The World Around Us provides an introduction to geography. It considers the world we live in and relates it to the child's immediate surroundings.

Book 2 A World of Movement illustrates how movement affects the physical and human environment through studies ranging from rivers to routes and journeys.

Book 3 A World of Change builds on the child's growing understanding of the family, neighbourhood and wider world by considering how places alter and develop.

Book 4 World Issues deals with more complex ideas to do with the environment and the way people interact with their surroundings.

One of the main aims of *World Watch* is to provide children with an overview of geography so that they have a framework for organising new knowledge and understanding as they proceed with their schooling.

The series also aims to develop enquiry skills. To make sense of the contemporary world children need to be able to interpret and analyse information.

Structure of the books

Each of the *World Watch* books is divided into ten units giving a balance between themes and places as follows:

Themes
Physical geography: Landscape, Water, Weather (3 units)
Human geography: Settlement, Transport/Communication, Work (3 units)
Environmental geography: Environment (1 unit)

Places
Locality studies: UK, Europe, World (3 units)
The locality studies bring together all the themes covered in the earlier units. The localities have been selected from around the world so that children are introduced to the different continents in turn.

Progression

Each book follows the same structure *(see page 5)* so it is possible to consider the main themes at different levels of complexity. For example in Book 1 the unit on Transport introduces children to different types of transport. In Book 2 the Transport unit looks at routes and journeys, while in Books 3 and 4 it consider changes and the development of modern technology. The opportunities for achieving progression are immediately apparent. At the same time there is scope for reinforcement and revisiting which will be particularly helpful for the less able child.

Mapwork

The *World Watch* books contain a range of maps and plans. These are included specifically to convey information about the places which are studied in the different units. Books 1 and 2 contain maps with pictorial representations of hills and mountains, while different relief colouring is used in Books 3 and 4. Aerial photos are included as appropriate with a progression from oblique angles to vertical overhead perspectives.

Cross-curricular links

Geography is a synthesis subject, uniquely placed between the sciences and the humanities. By structuring the books around clearly identified themes, links with other subjects are easier to make *(see page 7)*. For example, the units on Transport and Communication could be developed through work on history and science. These units also provide good opportunities for introducing information technology and cross-curricular themes such as environmental education and economic and industrial understanding.

THEMES and PLACES	Book 1 The World Around Us	Book 2 A World of Movement
Landscape	Planet Earth	The Seashore
Water	A Wet Planet	Rivers
Weather	Hot and Cold Places	Recording the Weather
Settlement	A Place to Live	Towns
Transport/ Communication	Ways of Travelling	Routes and Journeys
Work	Food and Farming	Making Things
Environment	Caring for the Countryside	Caring for Buildings
United Kingdom	Scotland	Northern Ireland
Europe	France	Germany
World	Asia - A village in India	North and Central America - A Caribbean island

Using the books

Whole school planning

World Watch has been designed to fit the requirements of whole school planning. Whole school planning is essential for continuity and progression. It helps to make teachers more confident and more involved in the schemes of work that they are using.

Following the scheme

World Watch is a progressive scheme which can be incorporated into a number of curriculum formats. Some schools may wish to follow the material in the same order that it is presented in the books. However, depending on the school plan, other teachers may wish to select individual units to support broad, cross-curricular topics *(see the Topic planner on page 7)*.

The *World Watch* books cover the requirements of the national curriculum. The themes balance physical, human and environmental geography, while the locality studies provide details of places and countries in the United Kingdom and the wider world including economically developing countries.

Mixed age classes

A significant number of junior schools now have classes which span two different year groups. *World Watch* is designed so that Books 1 and 2 can be used with the lower juniors, and Books 3 and 4 can be used with the upper juniors. If this approach is followed two modules each six terms long will need to be devised.

In some smaller village schools the age range within a class may be even wider. In these circumstances *World Watch* can be used as an individual scheme with appropriate study units selected according to the needs of the child. Discussion or activity work can be undertaken in groups or pairs *(see Differentiation on page 10)*.

Finding time for geography

Each unit in the *World Watch* books contains material for about three hours' work. Any practical investigations or enquiries in the local environment will require extra time.

Topic planner

This planner shows how you can link the material in Books 1 and 2 to a variety of different topics.

Topic	Units in Book 1	Units in Book 2
Where We Live	A Place to Live pp20-25	Towns pp20-25
Weather	Hot and Cold Places pp14-19	Recording the Weather pp14-19
Water	A Wet Planet pp8-13	Rivers pp8-13
Food	Food and Farming pp32-37 France pp50-53	
Environment	Caring for the Countryside pp38-43	Caring for Towns pp38-43
Jobs	Food and Farming pp32-37 France pp54-55	Making Things pp32-37
Transport/Journeys	Ways of Travelling pp26-31	Routes and Journeys pp26-31
Living Things	Caring for the Countryside pp38-43	The Seashore pp2-7
The Earth	Planet Earth pp2-7	The Seashore pp2-7
UK Locality	Scotland pp44-49	Northern Ireland pp44-49
European Study	France pp50-55	Germany pp50-55
Developing Countries	Asia pp56-61	North America pp58-61

Layout of the units

Thematic units

The thematic units all follow the same model and are divided into three double page spreads. The first spread serves as a stimulus, the second contains research material and the third highlights the opportunities for investigation.

Stimulus spreads
The stimulus spreads provide an introduction to the unit. Photographs and artwork are used to arouse the children's interest. The children are encouraged to discuss the material on the spread and to use appropriate geographical vocabulary.

Research spreads
The research spreads develop the unit theme and provide reference material. The children are encouraged to use the text, pictures and photographs in their own studies and investigations. Information from distant places and fact files make this spread especially wide ranging.

Investigation spreads
The investigation spreads explore the opportunities for enquiries and investigations. Examples of children's work are used to illustrate some of the possibilities. Local maps and plans are also included as they are a source of information.

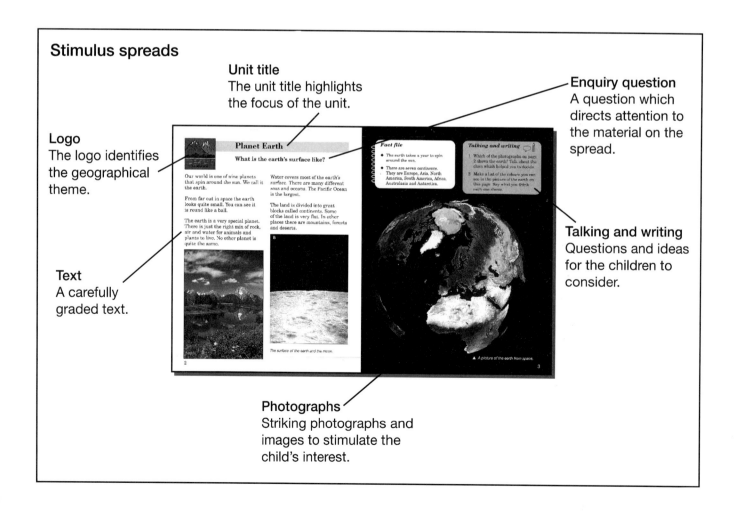

Research spreads

Introduction
The spread starts with an enquiry question and is followed by a short introductory text.

Diagrams and photographs
Diagrams and photographs for the children to interrogate.

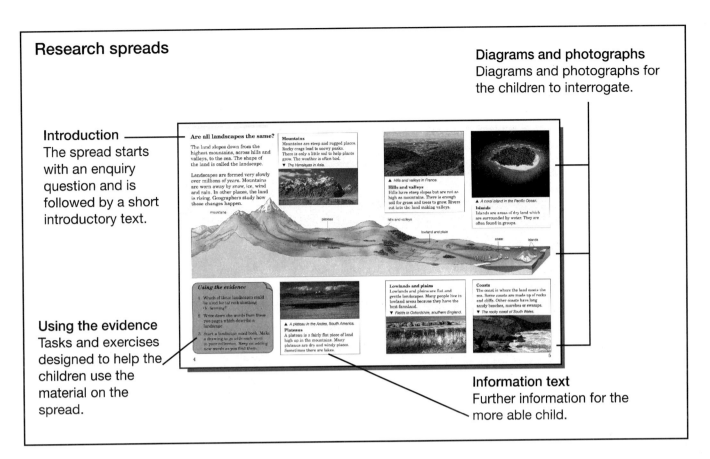

Using the evidence
Tasks and exercises designed to help the children use the material on the spread.

Information text
Further information for the more able child.

Investigation spreads

Introduction
A short description which relates the ideas in the unit to the child's own experience.

School projects
Examples of how to conduct local enquiries and investigations.

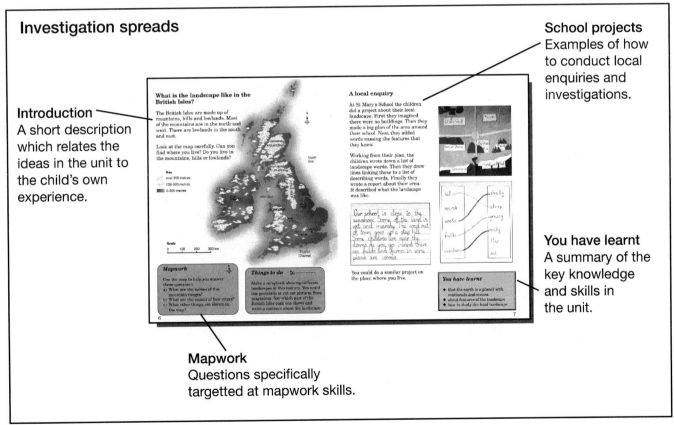

You have learnt
A summary of the key knowledge and skills in the unit.

Mapwork
Questions specifically targetted at mapwork skills.

Locality studies

The locality studies bring together the different themes covered in the earlier units and show how people interact with their surroundings. As well as including a study of places in the UK, Europe or the wider world, each locality study unit has an overview of the appropriate country or continent.

9

Differentiation

World Watch sets out to provide access to the curriculum to children of all abilities. It is structured so that children can respond to and use the material in a variety of ways. Within each unit there is a range of exercises and discussion questions. This means activities can be selected which are appropriate to individual circumstances.

Differentiation by outcome

The stimulus spreads emphasise the importance of talking and discussion and are designed to capture the children's imagination. There are opportunities for slow learners to relate the material to their own experience. More able children will be able to consider the underlying geographical concepts. The pace and range of the discussion can be controlled to suit the needs of the class or group.

Differentiation by task

The research spreads provide photographs and diagrams for the children to interpret. The exercises that are suggested can be used at a number of ability levels. More exercises could be added for slow learners. Classroom assistants can use the material with individual children or small groups. More able children can embark on their own investigations and research.

Differentiation by process

Children of all abilities benefit from exploring their environment and conducting their own investigations. The investigation spreads stress the importance of direct experience and firsthand learning. Work in the local area can overcome the problems of written communication by focusing on concrete events. There are also opportunities for using cameras, tape recorders and computers and presenting learning in a variety of ways such as lists, diagrams and written descriptions.

Differentiation checklist

1. Have I fully developed the opportunities for talking and discussion using the stimulus sections?
2. Have I identified and explained key geographical vocabulary?
3. Have I considered using the research sections in a number of different ways for children of mixed ability?
4. Have I used work in the local environment to support the work that the children are doing?
5. Have I used the extension ideas and the copymasters to develop specific skills?
6. Have I considered the advantages of group or paired work for slower children?
7. Have I displayed and exhibited the children's work so they can learn from each other and develop a corporate understanding of the unit?
8. Have I rewarded the children's achievement?
9. Have I used the 'You have learnt' box to check the children's knowledge and understanding?
10. Have I analysed the children's attainment to help select the best strategies for using the next unit?

Assessment

Schools are currently obliged to report on children's progress in geography each year and to assess the level they have attained at the end of each key stage. Most assessments will be made by the teacher. *World Watch* can help with this in a number of ways.

Demonstrating progress through the key stage

World Watch is structured around geographical themes which show a clear progression. These themes can be used as the basis for a record of attainment for individual children as they pass through the school.

Showing geographical understanding

Many geographical ideas require reasoning and understanding rather than responses which are simply right or wrong. One way of assessing these qualities is by focussing on the way the child uses geographical vocabulary. The language which is used in the books has been carefully chosen. There are also lists in the unit notes *(see pages 14-23)* which give the key words for the unit.

Ways of making an assessment

The variety of material in *World Watch* means that assessment can be conducted in different ways.

1. The stimulus spreads provide opportunities to listen to the child's spoken response.
2. The research spreads will build up into a folder of written work that indicates skills and abilities.
3. The investigation spreads allow the teacher to observe children conducting their own investigations.
4. The 'You have learnt' boxes provide the basis for formal recall, either orally or through tests.
5. The copymasters *(see pages 26-45)* can be used diagnostically and can be used to show specific accomplishments at set points in the year.

Providing evidence

As children work through *World Watch* they will build up a folder of work on different themes and places. This will include mapwork and investigations in the local area which will provide evidence of breadth, progression and achievement in geography.

Reporting to parents

Parents want to know what their children can do and how they compare with others. Using work from the *World Watch* scheme teachers can report on what the class has done and whether an individual child has been above average, satisfactory or is in need of help.

Studying the local area

The local area is the immediate vicinity around the school and the home. It consists of three different components: the school building, the school grounds, and local streets and buildings. By studying their local area children will learn about the different features which make their environment distinctive and how it attains a specific character. When they are familiar with their own area they will then be able to make meaningful comparisons with more distant places.

There are many opportunities to combine *World Watch* with practical work in the local area *(see the investigation pages of the pupil books for examples)*. Firsthand experience is fundamental to good practice in geography teaching and a clear requirement in the programme of study. The local area can be used not only to develop ideas from human geography but also to illustrate physical and environmental themes. The checklist below illustrates some of the features which could be identified and studied.

Landscape features	Hills, valleys, cliffs, mountains, woods
Water features	Stream, pond, lake, river, estuary, coast
Surface features	Slopes, rock, soil, plants and other small scale features
Climate features	Sites for work on micro-climate (usually school grounds)
Settlement	Sites showing origins of settlement (crossing point, route centre, castle)
Buildings	House, cottage, terrace, flats, housing estate
Transport	Bus station, railway station, airport, harbour, roads (safe places for traffic surveys)
Industry	Farm, workshop, warehouse, factory, offices
Shops	Single shop, shopping parade, shopping mall, supermarket, hypermarket
Services	Fire, police, ambulance, hospital, dentist, recycling point
Leisure facilities	Library, museum, park, swimming pool, golf course, leisure centre
Local issues	Pedestrianisation, improvement scheme, new shops, play areas, road widening, new reservoir, rubbish tip

All work in the local area involves collecting and analysing information. An important way in which this can be achieved is through the use of maps and plans. Other techniques include annotated drawings, bar charts, tables and reports. The skills used in each unit are listed in the unit notes *(see pages 14-23)*.

Studying contrasting and distant localities

World Watch Book 1 contains studies of the following places in the UK:

pp24-25   A village in Kent (Worth)
pp30   A suburb in the West Midlands (Quarry Bank)
pp32-33   A farm in Dorset (Brimley Farm)
pp46-47   A city in Scotland (Edinburgh)
pp48-49   An island community (Isle of Mull)

The overseas place studies in Book 1 are:

pp52-53   A farming community in France (Parnac in the Dordogne)
pp54-55   A Paris suburb (Flins near Mantes-la-Jolie)
pp59-61   A village in India (Pallipadu near Madras on the east coast)

The place studies focus on people and describe named families and children. By considering small scale environments and everyday life the information is presented at a scale which children can understand. Research shows that children reach a peak of friendliness towards other countries and nations at about the age of ten. It is important to capitalise on this educationally and to challenge prejudices and stereotypes.

Coverage of photographs in Book 1

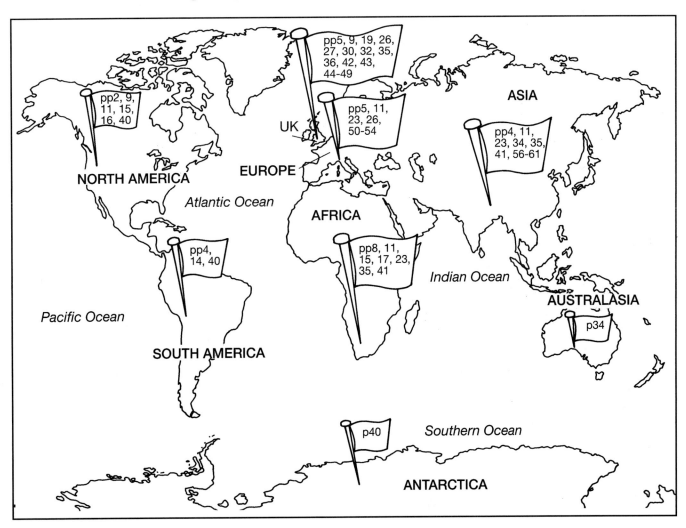

Information on the units

Landscape: Planet Earth

The word 'geography' literally means 'earth writing'. The way that wind, water, ice and snow have worn away the land is part of the story. The way people have responded to their physical surroundings is the other major strand.

The earth has a fixed orbit around the sun and has a relatively stable climate. The surface is covered with a mixture of rock, air and water. These unique conditions enabled life to evolve. The first organisms probably date back 3,000 million years. On this timescale human beings are very recent additions as they have only emerged in the last 500,000 years.

Stimulus

What is the earth's surface like? pp 2-3

- Photograph A shows the earth's surface (West Teton Park, Wyoming, USA). The most striking features are the blue sky, the snow-covered mountains, the grass, the trees and the lake. Photograph B shows the surface of the moon. It is dry and dusty and there are craters where meteors have crashed to the ground.

- The satellite photograph on page 3 has been given false colours to represent different types of vegetation and landscape. White is used for ice and high mountains, yellow for deserts, green for fields and forests, purple for the tundra and blue for water. Do not take it for granted that young children readily perceive the earth as a globe. Explore their idea of what they think our planet is like.

Research

Are all landscapes the same? pp 4-5

- The earth's crust has been shaped over geological time by a complex variety of forces - violent movements, ageing of the rocks, the action of water and erosion. At this stage it is enough for children to be able to identify different types of landscape and to interpret the photographs.

- One of the main aims of this spread is to develop vocabulary. Children need to know the names of specific landscape features. The landscape word book will help them to remember different terms. The characteristics of the landscapes will be revealed particularly vividly when the children associate the photographs with human activity.

Investigation

What is the landscape like in the British Isles? pp 6-7

- The pictorial map of the British Isles contains the main physical features of the British Isles.

- The scrapbook exercise on page 6 is designed to encourage children to use the new vocabulary that they have acquired, otherwise they are likely to forget it.

- It is important for the children to make a study of physical features in the place where they live, as outlined on page 7. This will help them to develop enquiry skills and will enhance their sense of place.

Key vocabulary

coast	hill	mountain
crag	island	planet
desert	landscape	plateau
forest	lowland	valley

Main skills

Interpreting photographs
Using a cross-section diagram
Developing geographical language

Copymasters See ❶ and ❷ : Planet Earth

Water: A Wet Planet

Water has a profound influence on our environment. Seas and oceans cover large parts of the earth's surface. At the poles there are massive sheets of ice which never melt. Most of the water in the world is either salty or frozen. This only leaves a very small portion of fresh water.

People depend on fresh water for their survival. It is essential for drinking, cooking and washing. Modern industry and agriculture also require large quantities of water in order to operate. In some places, water is used to generate hydro-electric power. Elsewhere it is used for irrigation. Where rivers are deep enough they are used by ships and boats. Of all the varied resources on the earth's surface, water is arguably one of the most important.

Stimulus

Where do we find water? pp 8-9

- The photograph of the Victoria Falls introduces the unit in a dramatic way. As well as making a collection of 'water words' you could get the children to write their own poems about rivers and water.

- You will need to discuss the relationship between ice, water and steam and how this relates to temperature. As the temperature rises, ice melts and turns into a liquid. When a liquid is heated it boils and turns into a gas. As the temperature falls the gas condenses into a liquid and solidifies into ice.

- The diagram on page 9 illustrates some of the different forms that water can take. It is particularly hard for young children to appreciate that water vapour is an invisible gas. Just as a nought in mathematics is a crucial part of a counting scale so it is highly significant that the air contains invisible vapour.

- The photographs show a reservoir in the UK (top left), a river in Austria (bottom left) and a glacier and an iceberg in Greenland (top and bottom right).

Research

Why is water important? p 10

- The picture on page 10 illustrates how a range of plants and animals depend on water for their survival. The children could consider what other examples might be included in the picture. Water pollution can be introduced to provide a link to wider environmental issues.

Using water p 11

- Wherever people live they need water. The photographs on page 11 show water use scenes from around the world: Kenya (top left), Roumania (top right), USA (bottom left) and China (bottom right). The children can use them to compare with their own experience.

Investigation

How is water shown on maps? pp 12-13

- Water features are shown on most maps and they are an important part of the landscape. The exercise on page 12 is also a useful way of introducing young children to maps and simple co-ordinates in a meaningful context.

- From an early age children will have noticed water running down window panes and across roads and slopes. The investigation work suggested on page 13 builds on this experience and leads children to recognise part of the water cycle sequence. (The water cycle is dealt with fully in Book 3.) You might also discuss evaporation, bearing in mind it is an idea that children will need to revisit.

Key vocabulary				**Main skills**
gas	lake	reservoir	stream	Recognising water in different forms
glacier	liquid	slopes	waterfall	Using co-ordinates on a map
iceberg	marsh	solid	water vapour	Making fieldwork sketches

Copymasters See ❸ and ❹ : A Wet Planet

Weather: Hot and Cold Places

There are great variations in weather around the world. The hottest places are in deserts like the Sahara where clear skies allow fierce sunlight to reach the surface. At the equator the air pressure is generally lower giving rise to heavy rainfall and humid weather. The interior of Antarctica is particularly cold, partly because it is high above sea level and partly because it lacks the moderating influence of the sea.

Fact file

Hottest place	Al'Aziziyah, Libya (1922): 58°C
Coldest place	Vostock, Antarctica (1988): -88°C
Wettest place	Tutundendo, Colombia: 11,770mm average annual rainfall
Driest place	Atacama desert, Chile: no rain for several hundred years

Stimulus

Is the weather the same all over the world? pp 14-15

- You will probably find it best to talk about the weather in different places rather than the climate. The notion of climate depends on understanding averages which is conceptually difficult for young children.

- The photographs on this spread (Amazon rainforest, Sahara desert and Greenland) illustrate how the weather affects plant and animal life.

- Plants and animals have been able to adapt to different climates over long periods of time. People, on the other hand, use technology to help them survive in challenging conditions. This contrast is something which the children should discuss as they consider the questions on page 15.

Research

How do people live in hot and cold places? pp 16-17

- The interaction between people and the environment is central to the study of geography. It can be seen particularly clearly where the weather conditions are harsh, as in the desert and polar lands.

- The photograph and drawings of the oasis provide a range of study material. Children could compile a similar study for the coast of Greenland. The world map on page 18 is an extra resource which may be used in this work.

- The photographs on page 16 show the harbour of a fishing village and fish drying in Greenland.

Investigation

Why are some places hot and other places cold? pp 18-19

- The diagram on page 18 illustrates how the sun's rays pass through more atmosphere and are spread over a greater surface area in the polar lands than at the equator. You will need to discuss this with the children.

- The world map shows the distribution of rainforest, desert and polar climates. Note that the hottest places on earth are the deserts north and south of the equator and not in the rainforests.

- The material on page 19 is designed to relate hot and cold climates to the children's own experiences and to encourage school-based work. The children could record hot and cold places on a plan of the school as an extension exercise.

Key vocabulary

climate	oasis	Antarctica
desert	polar lands	Greenland
equator	rainforest	Sahara desert

Main skills

Extracting information from photographs
Making comparisons
Reading a map

Copymasters See ❺ and ❻ : Hot and Cold Places

Settlement: A Place to Live

All the villages in Britain had been founded by the Norman conquest in 1066. The sites that were chosen reflect a variety of different needs such as food, shelter, communication and defence. In some country areas, fresh water came to the surface in springs along a particular contour line giving rise to a row of villages. Around the coast, fishing villages were built to take advantage of natural features such as harbours.

Nowadays the traditional interaction between people and their physical surroundings has been superceded by economic forces. Many of the people who live in villages have jobs in nearby towns and cities. Others have decided to retire to the countryside. The result is that there have been irreversible changes in rural life.

Stimulus

What is a settlement? pp 20-21
- The stimulus picture highlights the different elements which make up a settlement by using a picture of how people might colonise another planet.
- The children should be encouraged to relate the land use map on page 20 to the various features shown in the picture. Some children will only be able to name individual buildings and structures. As they mature they come to recognise the relationship and purpose of buildings within a settlement.

Research

What is a village? pp 22-23
- The study of Bainbridge in North Yorkshire shows how people have made use of their physical surroundings (the Pennines) in a real life situation.
- All over the world people build houses to provide shelter. The photographs illustrate how weather and landscape influence the design of settlements around the world.

Investigation

How are villages in the United Kingdom changing? pp 24-25
- All settlements change over a period of time. The place study of Worth in Kent shows how the old village around the green has been extended towards the main road.
- You might decide to make a similar study of a village in your own area. A large scale map (1:1,250) will provide most of the background information that you need. If you can take photographs of the main geographical features while you are on the visit you will be able to use these when you return to the classroom.
- Children find it hard to distinguish between old and new buildings and are often misled by superficial clues such as peeling paintwork or imitation lead windows. The evidence from old maps and documents is crucial in supporting fieldwork observations.

Key vocabulary

change	materials	shelter
countryside	planet	surroundings
features	safety	survival
land use	settlement	village

Main skills

Making deductions
Interpreting an annotated drawing
Identifying features on a map

Copymasters See ❼ and ❽ : A Place to Live

Transport: Ways of Travelling

One of the features of the modern world is that people are travelling further and at greater speeds than ever before. In the 1930s, for example, it used to take 16 days to travel from Britain to Barbados by sea. The same journey can now be done in eight hours by air.

Good communications are essential to modern economic activity. Grain and foodstuffs are grown in one country and transported to another. Oil from the Middle East provides power for industries thousands of kilometres away. Tropical islands have become popular holiday destinations for Europeans.

In Britain the rise in private car ownership in the last 30 years has meant that people are making more journeys and are travelling further by car (*see table below*).

	1961	1971	1981	1991
Air	1	2	3	5
Rail	38	35	34	38
Road				
(public vehicles)	69	56	49	45
(private vehicles)	160	338	411	601
(million passenger kilometres)				

Source: *Annual Abstract of Stastics* (HMSO)

Stimulus

What different types of transport are there? pp 26-27

- The collage of pictures on pages 26 and 27 brings together the diverse perceptions that children have of transport. Although the technology has changed over the past 150 years, the effect of transport on people and the environment is basically the same.

- It is impossible to say which of the four types of transport is best as they each have strengths and weaknesses. The nature of the terrain, the type of the load, the distance to be travelled and need for speed are some of the factors which the children might consider.

Research

How are people and goods carried from place to place? pp 28-29

- The drawing and notes about the airport describe the infrastructure needed for air travel. You could get the children to discuss the infrastructure needed for road, rail and water transport.

- The cross-section drawings on page 29 are designed to promote further research and investigations in different vehicles and the way that they work.

Investigation

A local investigation in the West Midlands pp 30-31

- Roads, railways and other transport facilities are significant features in all parts of the country. It is possible to identify and classify them simply by working from a map.

- Ideally you should organise some work in the local environment which will enable the children to make practical studies of their own.

- The purpose of the transport files is to indicate what type of transport is likely to be passing through any particular area.

Key vocabulary
aeroplane   goods   track
airport   harbour   transport
container   load   travel
ferry   tanker   vehicle

Main skills
Using a cross-section diagram
Reading a map
Using a data file

Copymasters See ❾ and ❿ : Ways of Travelling

Work: Food and Farming

There have been great changes in agriculture over the past 50 years. The increased use of machinery, fertilisers and insecticides have led to much higher yields and greater productivity. As a result, Britain can now meet 60 per cent of its own needs. Many countries in the developing world are self-sufficient in food despite rapid increases in their populations.

However these benefits have only been achieved at a price. We now realise that intensive farming leads to long-term pollution problems and can cause soil degradation. There are also serious problems associated with the present system of world agriculture in which poor countries supply richer ones with cash crops at low prices. This had led to a downward spiral of poverty and increasing global inequalities.

Farm land in Britain is used as follows:

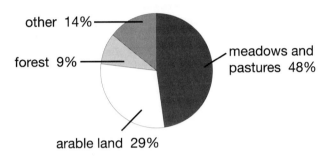

Stimulus

What is a farm? pp 32-33
- Brimley Farm in Dorset has been selected for this study because it is a mixed farm, while many other farms in the UK now specialise in crops, cattle or sheep.
- Children tend to have a rather romantic view of farming. Poems, songs and fairy tales overlook the fact that growing crops and looking after animals is a demanding occupation requiring long hours of repetitive work. The Talking and writing question introduces this idea. You might also discuss the pattern of seasonal activity.

Research

Are all farms the same? pp 34-35
- In many parts of the world farmers tend small plots and grow food for their everyday needs. However crops which are exported are often grown on plantations where large areas of land are all used in the same way.
- The text beside the photographs stresses the relationship between the different plants and the climates in which they grow. This develops the ideas in the unit on the weather *(see Hot and Cold Places pages 14-19)*. It is important that the children use specialist terms such as orchard, ranch, estate and plantation.

Investigation

Why are there different types of farm in the British Isles? p 36
- The climate is arguably the single most important influence on farming. This explains why sheep and dairying predominate in the wetter, western parts of the UK, while crops like wheat are grown in the sunnier east.

Where does our food come from? p 37
- If you are able to visit a greengrocer's shop, you could find out about the origins of fruit and vegetables at first hand.

Key vocabulary
barley   estate   plough
cacao   maize   product
crop   orchard   ranch
dairy farm plantation wheat

Main skills
Reading for information
Interpreting a map
Setting up a display

Copymasters See ⑪ and ⑫ : Food and Farming

Environment: Caring for the Countryside

During this century there has been an enormous expansion of industry and population around the world. The discovery of nuclear fission, the use of electricity and other technological innovations have brought immense changes. For the first time in history people now have the ability to influence the balance of life on earth.

This new power has brought with it the realisation that the earth is a fragile planet. Either we live in harmony with our surroundings or we exploit them and ignore the future. Environmentalists have made it clear that the earth is the only home we have. Whatever decision we take, the children who are now at school will have to live with the consequences.

The bar chart below shows the types of things people do to help the environment.

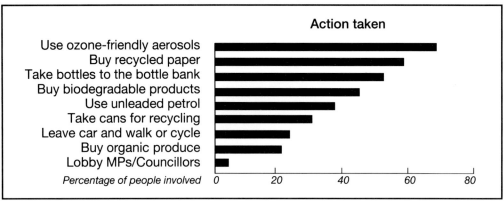

Source: Department of the Enviroment

Stimulus

What is a habitat? pp 38-39
- The picture shows how a piece of undisturbed wasteland can be a valuable habitat.
- In order to decide where each animal would live, the children will have to discuss what each one needs. Some animals live in damp, shady places for protection. Others prefer dry, sunny places. The children may be able to find several suitable sites in the picture.

Research

What are people doing to care for plants and animals? pp 40-41
- Many young children are surprisingly well informed about environmental problems. This double page spread takes a global perspective and identifies problems from around the world.
- The photographs illustrate how people are trying to solve environmental problems. It is vital that we take a positive perspective and do not leave children feeling powerless in the face of overwhelming difficulties.

Investigation

Nature reserves p 42
- This page shows one of the ways people are caring for the environment in this country. There may be reserves in your own area that you could investigate.

Improving the school grounds p 43
- There are many small scale improvement projects which can be undertaken even within the school grounds. Children in urban areas are not always aware that plants and animals also live in cities. The photographs illustrate different habitats and extend the ideas from pages 38 and 39.

Key vocabulary

			Main skills
animal	national park	reserve	Making judgements
environment	plant	shelter	Designing a poster
extinct	pollution	wasteground	Using imagination
habitat	protect	wilderness	

Copymasters See ⓭ and ⓮ : Caring for the Countryside

United Kingdom: Scotland

Scotland has a third of the total land area of the UK with a population of 5.1 million (less than 10 per cent of the total UK population). Within Scotland there are marked regional variations with most activity concentrated in the central lowlands.

Since the 1970s Scotland has developed as the centre for the North Sea oil industry. This has helped to replace traditional heavy industries such as iron, steel, coal mining and ship building. Ski resorts and conifer plantations are important new developments in the countryside. There has also been growing support for Scottish nationalism.

Overview

What is Scotland like? pp 44-45

- Before studying specific localities, the children need to be aware of the environment in which they are set. This double page spread provides a general introduction to Scotland with information on both physical and human geography.

- If your school is in Scotland you might use this spread to help you to deliver some of the specific requirements of the Environmental Studies curriculum. If your school is outside Scotland, the map, photographs and text will serve to expand the children's ideas of another part of the United Kingdom.

Locality studies

Edinburgh - the capital city of Scotland pp 46-47

- The introduction explains in simple terms why Edinburgh occupies its present site. The growth of settlements involves both a historical and geographical dimension. This is something which is explored in greater detail in World Watch Book 2.

- The words and pictures highlight some of the features which give Edinburgh its character. The ancient buildings and landscape setting are particularly noteworthy but children also need to understand that modern cities have a wide range of facilities.

- Arthur's Seat and the rock on which Edinburgh castle is built are old volcanoes which were active 325 million years ago but are now extinct. More information on volcanoes is given in Book 3.

Mull - an island on the west coast of Scotland pp 48-49

- Some children will have been to an island on their holidays and will be able to identify with Roy and Christine. However you should also make sure that the rest of the class know what an island is. The fact that Roy and Christine have to travel by ferry and that the map shows Mull surrounded by water are important clues.

- The west coast of Scotland provides a distinctive and valuable habitat for plants and animals. You could use the information about Mull as part of a project on the environment. The Caring for the Countryside unit (*see pages 38-43*) considers the idea of habitat in greater detail and provides a natural link.

Key vocabulary

cliffs	holiday	offices
croft	island	oil rig
ferry	lowland	Scotland
forestry	moors	tourism

Main skills

Making a fact file
Following a route on a plan
Comparing different places
Drawing a map

Copymasters See ⑮ and ⑯ : Scotland

Europe: France

After the Ukraine, France is the second largest country in Europe with a population of 56 million people. About one-fifth of the population live in the largest city - Paris. The Rhône valley forms an important corridor for road and rail transport to and from the south.

France is in the forefront of modern technology. A network of high speed railway lines is being built linking Paris and the Channel Tunnel with other cities and European capitals. Over half of the country's electricity comes from nuclear energy and many new high-tech industries have been set up, particularly around Grenoble and Toulouse. However France also has a strong agricultural base. It is a major producer of wheat, beef and dairy products and it has one of the largest wine industries in the world.

Overview

What is France like? pp 50-51

- You might begin by getting the children to say what they know about France. Do not be worried if some of the answers are crude stereotypes. Their ideas will become more refined as they study the unit.

- The map of France on page 50 shows physical features and major cities. It is valuable to discuss the shape of the country, the location of the cities and the position of France in relation to the UK. Parnac and Flins are marked because they are studied in the rest of the unit.

- When the children answer the question on page 51 they should use information from the map and photographs as well as the text.

Locality studies

The French countryside pp 52-53

- The photograph shows the village of Parnac (population 377) and the surrounding countryside. It contains a lot of information which the children can discuss. Remember to consider the physical setting in a river valley as well as the crops and vegetation. You could also discuss what the weather is like and the probable time of year.

- When the children have listed the food that grows around Parnac, you might make a comparison with the food that is produced in your own area. What is the reason for the differences? You might find it useful to refer to the unit on Food and Farming (*see pages 32-37*).

The Renault Clio pp 54-55

- In the past it was relatively easy to say where goods were manufactured. Now they are often assembled from units made in different locations. Renault has factories in other parts of Europe (Spain, Portugal, Belgium and Slovenia) as well as in other parts of the world. The Clio is assembled at Flins but many of the components are made elsewhere.

- Although young children know that we have to pay for the things we buy, they find it hard to realise what the shopkeeper does with the money. The money diagram is designed to extend their understanding. This will prepare them for the question about what would happen if people stopped buying the Renault Clio.

Key vocabulary

chemicals	factory	skiing
climate	industry	supermarket
crops	maize	village
Europe	pâté	walnuts

Main skills

Making a list
Finding places on a map
Making deductions

Copymasters See ⑰ and ⑱ : France

World: Asia

Three-fifths of the people in the world live in Asia. There are over 1,100 million Chinese, and India has a population of 850 million. However Asia is such a vast continent that large areas are almost completely uninhabited, particularly in the mountains of China and Tibet, and the plains of Siberia.

Most of the countries of Asia are economically underdeveloped. However cities are growing fast and there are considerable problems in coping with the pace of change. Japan and Korea are notable exceptions. In some countries, like Russia, there are huge pressures on the environment. It is estimated that contamination from toxic waste has made almost one-sixth of the land in Russia uninhabitable.

Overviews

What is Asia like? pp 56-57

- Children find it hard to distinguish between Europe and Asia because they are physically joined together. The Ural mountains form the main barrier between the two, although it is not important to identify the exact boundary with young children.

- The map and photographs are designed to promote discussion and to show contrasting landscapes and environments which the children can visualise.

- Before the children make the poster it is valuable for them to discuss who it might be aimed at and what it might contain.

India - a country in Asia p 58

- In many ways India reflects the scale and diversity of Asia itself. This is something which will emerge as the children make the zigzag book.

- Children often get confused between cities, countries and continents. This is because they think of them as separate categories of equal importance. They will grasp the correct relationship when they realise that cities, countries and continents 'fit into each other' in a hierarchy. However this understanding only comes with increasing age and maturity.

Locality study

Pallipadu - a village in India pp 59-61

- The study of Pallipadu provides information about physical and human geography and the changes that are taking place in the village. It is important to consider these different elements when making a locality study.

- The exercises on page 61 encourage children to think about the positive aspects of life in Pallipadu in order to counteract any negative images of India they may have acquired from the media.

Key vocabulary

capital festival Asia
cement monsoon Gobi desert
continent plain Himalayan mountains
cyclone rainforest Siberia

Main skills
Interpreting photographs
Reading a map
Making comparisons

Copymasters See ⑲ and ⑳ : Asia

Copymaster matrix

Theme	Copymaster	Description
Landscape	1 Planet Earth	The children make drawings of four different landscapes and link them to a diagram.
	2 Planet Earth	The children complete four pictures to show activities in a landscape context.
Water	3 A Wet Planet	The children make drawings of an iceberg, snow, sea, rain and a lake.
	4 A Wet Planet	Working from labelled pictures, the children create a flow diagram.
Weather	5 Hot and Cold Places	The children colour and compare pictures of the desert, rainforest and polar lands.
	6 Hot and Cold Places	The children annotate a drawing of a scene from the polar lands.
Settlement	7 A Place to Live	Working from a plan, the children identify different features of a West African village.
	8 A Place to Live	The children make their own plan of a village using pictures of buildings and other features.
Transport	9 Ways of Travelling	The children draw different vehicles in the places they think they belong.
	10 Ways of Travelling	The children draw the appropriate vehicle round pictures of different cargoes.
Work	11 Food and Farming	The children add labels to a seasonal dial of farming activities.
	12 Food and Farming	The children link different products to the correct place on the world map.
Environment	13 Caring for the Countryside	The children consider where different living things might be found around their school.
	14 Caring for the Countryside	Working from a plan, the children list what they could see in different habitats.
United Kingdom	15 Scotland	The children cut out three picture strips to create a silhouette of the Edinburgh skyline.
	16 Scotland	The children draw lines linking pictures and labels to the map of Mull.
Europe	17 France	Using a map of Western Europe, the children colour France and name some key features.
	18 France	The children make up a fact file listing information about France.
World	19 Asia	The children complete a map of Asia showing the main landscape features.
	20 Asia	The children locate different features on a map of Pallipadu village, India.

Aim	Teaching Points
To reinforce recognition of important landscape features.	The children could either make up their own pictures or work from the pupil book.
To illustrate the connection between human and physical geography.	You could extend this activity by making a display of how people use the landscape.
To show that water can be a liquid, solid or gas.	None of the pictures show water as a gas because water vapour is invisible.
To show what happens to rainwater when it reaches the ground.	You will need to provide the children with scissors, glue and strips of paper.
To compare the weather in different places.	You may need to discuss the answers to the question with the children.
To help children identify features in a photograph.	Ask the children to annotate a drawing of the desert photo as an extension exercise.
To help children relate a photograph and plan of the same place.	Check that the children understand the different elements of the plan.
To reinforce the idea of a village.	It is important that the children draw the roads before they glue down the pictures.
To show why different types of transport are needed.	Read the children a picture book story about a journey as an extension activity.
To illustrate that vehicles have different purposes.	Get the children to set up a display of different toy vehicles.
To illustrate how farming depends on the weather.	The children could cut out their dials for a class display.
To develop the children's knowledge of the world map.	You may need to discuss the location of the UK on the map.
To promote first hand exploration of the immediate environment.	There are opportunities for extending the work into a study of minibeasts.
To encourage children to make a trail of their own.	You will need to allow plenty of time for the children to complete their work.
To introduce children to the idea of a silhouette.	The children will need scissors and Sellotape for this activity.
To highlight the features which make the Isle of Mull distinctive.	Check that the children understand the symbols on the map.
To help children recognise the shape and position of France on a map.	Extend the work by getting children to add features on their own map of France.
To give children practice in extracting information from a written text.	The information for the fact file could come from any of the pages in this unit.
To develop children's locational knowledge.	See that the children understand what the map shows before starting this exercise.
To get children to interrogate a large scale plan.	Ask the children to list the landmarks Vijaya would see on different routes.

❶ Planet Earth

Name _____

1. Draw a line from each box to the right place on the diagram.
2. Draw a landscape picture in each box.
3. Colour the pictures you have drawn.

mountains	coast

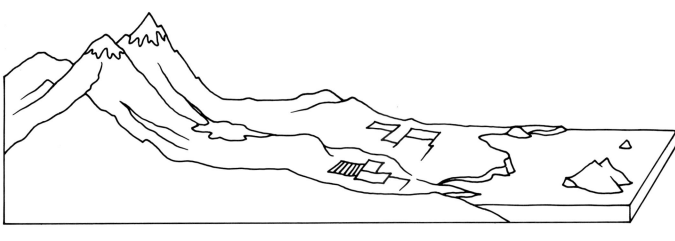

hills and valleys	island

World Watch 1: **Landscape** pp4-5 © Collins Educational 1994

② Planet Earth   Name _____

1. Draw a landscape around each of these picture.
2. Write the words where they belong.

   mountain   hills and valley   lowland   coast

World Watch 1: **Landscape** pp4-5

③ A Wet Planet

Name _____

1. Draw a picture to match the word at the top of each box.
2. Is the water in each picture a solid, a liquid or a gas? Tick the right box.

Iceberg

liquid ☐   solid ☐   gas ☐

Snow

liquid ☐   solid ☐   gas ☐

Sea

liquid ☐   solid ☐   gas ☐

Rain

liquid ☐   solid ☐   gas ☐

Lake

liquid ☐   solid ☐   gas ☐

4 A Wet Planet

Name _____

1. Read the sentences and colour the pictures.
2. Cut them out.
3. Glue the pictures in the right order on a strip of paper.
4. Draw arrows to join the pictures together.

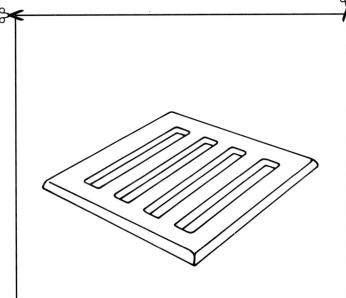

The water goes into the drain.

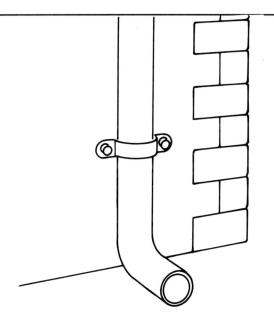

It flows down the downpipe.

Rain falls from clouds.

It runs off the roof into the gutter.

World Watch 1: Water p13 © Collins Educational 1994

⑤ Hot and Cold Places

Name _____

1 Colour the pictures.

2 What colours did you use? Finish these sentences.

I used................ for the desert because ....

I used................ for the polar lands because ....

I used................ for the rainforest because ....

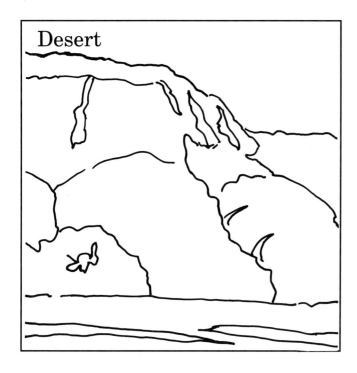
Desert

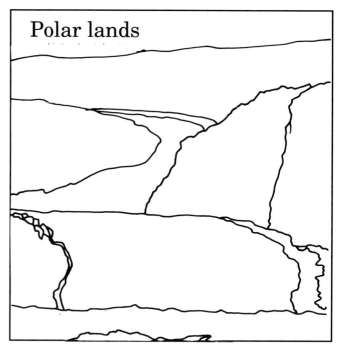
Polar lands

Rainforest

World Watch 1: **Weather** pp14–15

© Collins Educational 1994

6 Hot and Cold Places

Name _____

1 Write the words in the correct box around the picture.

snowy mountains   bare, rocky slopes
floating ice   thick clothes   fishing boats

2 What things are the same in this country? What things are different? Write a few sentences on a piece of paper.

7 A Place to Live

Name _____

1. Colour the boxes in the key.
2. Colour the plan of the village in Burkina Faso using the colours in the key.

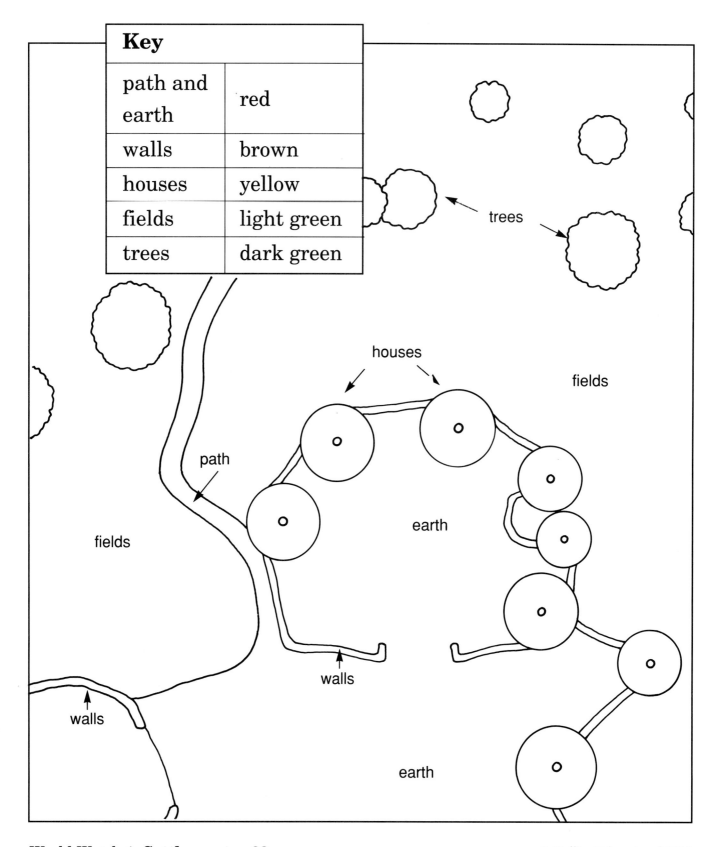

Key	
path and earth	red
walls	brown
houses	yellow
fields	light green
trees	dark green

World Watch 1: **Settlement** p23 © Collins Educational 1994

8 A Place to Live

Name _____

1. Colour the pictures.
2. Cut out the boxes.
3. Arrange the pictures on a piece of paper to make a village with roads and buildings.
4. Glue the pictures down.
5. Add some more drawings.

farmhouse | pond | inn

school | church | shop

bungalow | modern house | terraced houses

World Watch 1: **Settlement** pp24–25 © Collins Educational 1994

9 Ways of Travelling

Name _____

1 Draw the right vehicles on the pictures below.

ferry   plane   bus   train

World Watch 1: **Transport** pp26-27

© Collins Educational 1994

10 Ways of Travelling   Name _____

1. Which vehicle would carry the cargoes in the pictures below?
   ship   train   lorry

2. Draw the right shape around each cargo to finish the picture.

Which vehicle carries oil? _____

Which vehicle carries coal? _____

Which vehicle carries containers? _____

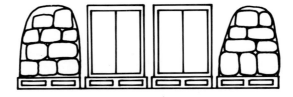

World Watch 1: **Transport** p29   © Collins Educational 1994

⑪ Food and Farming

Name _____

1. What is happening in each picture? Write the farming activity around the edge of the circle.

    cutting hedges   rolling grass   ploughing   harvesting crops

2. Write the name of the season in the empty boxes.

    spring   summer   autumn   winter

3. Colour the pictures.

World Watch 1: **Work** pp32–33

© Collins Educational 1994

Food and Farming   Name _____

1. Write the words where they belong under each picture.
   cattle   tea   rice   cacao   apples
2. Draw a line from each box to the right place on the map.
3. Draw a British farm product in the empty box.
4. Name your product and link it to the right place on the map.

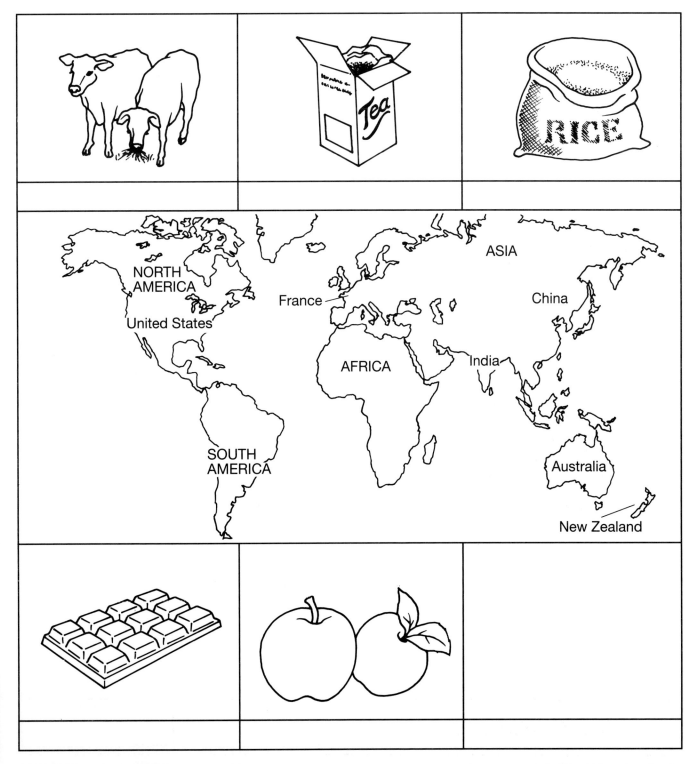

World Watch 1: **Work**   pp34–35

Caring for the Countryside   Name _____

1. Write the names under the pictures.
    worm   daisy   snail   woodlouse   spider
2. Where might each thing live around your school?
3. Visit the places to find out if you were right.
4. Circle 'yes' or 'no' to show your answer.

Living thing	Places where it might live (habitat)	Can I find it?
		Yes / No
		Yes / No
		Yes / No
		Yes / No
		Yes / No

World Watch 1: **Environment**   pp38-39

Caring for the Countryside Name _____

1. Write down the animals you might see on the trail.

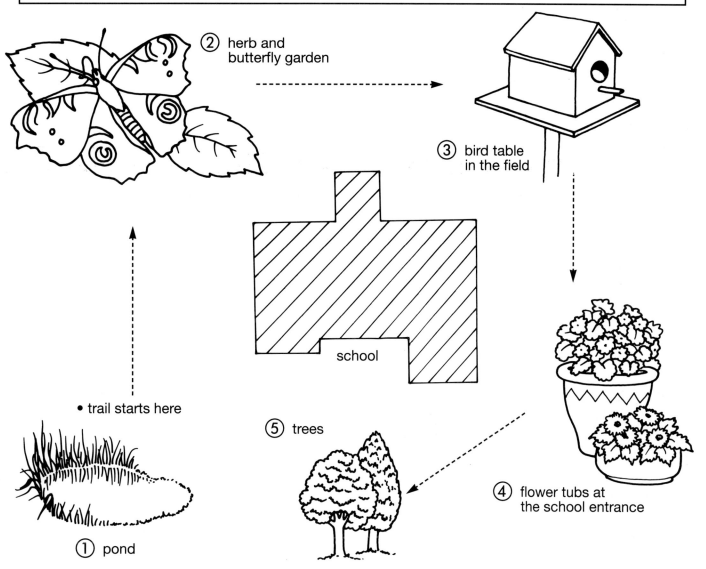

Stop	What animals might you see at this place?
1	
2	
3	
4	
5	

2. Make a list of different habitats in your school.
3. Work out a trail that links these places together.

World Watch 1: **Environment** p43 © Collins Educational 1994

⑮ Scotland

Name _____

1. Cut out the three silhouettes.
2. Join them together in the order they appear on the Edinburgh skyline.
3. Label the landmarks.

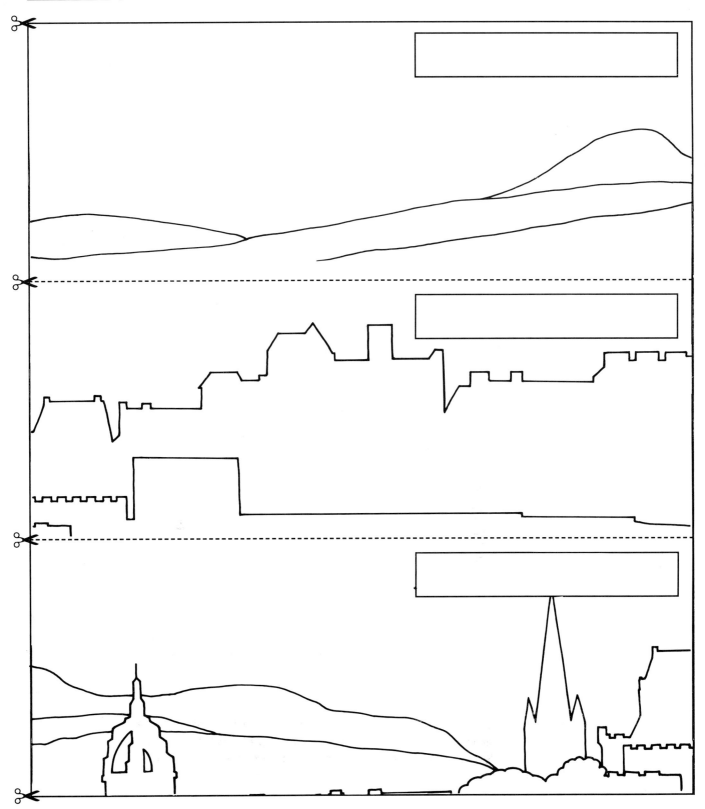

World Watch 1: **United Kingdom** pp46-47 © Collins Educational 1994

16 Scotland

Name _____

1. Draw a line from each picture to its symbol on the map.
2. Draw a line from each symbol to the right label in the box.

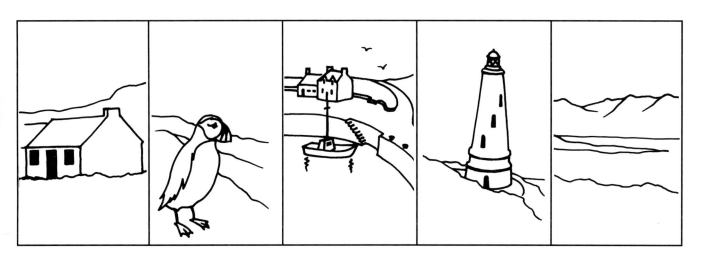

| puffin | mountain | croft | harbour | lighthouse |

World Watch 1: **United Kingdom** pp48-49 © Collins Educational 1994

17 France

Name _____

1. Colour the boxes in the key.
2. Colour the map using these colours.
3. Write in the missing names.

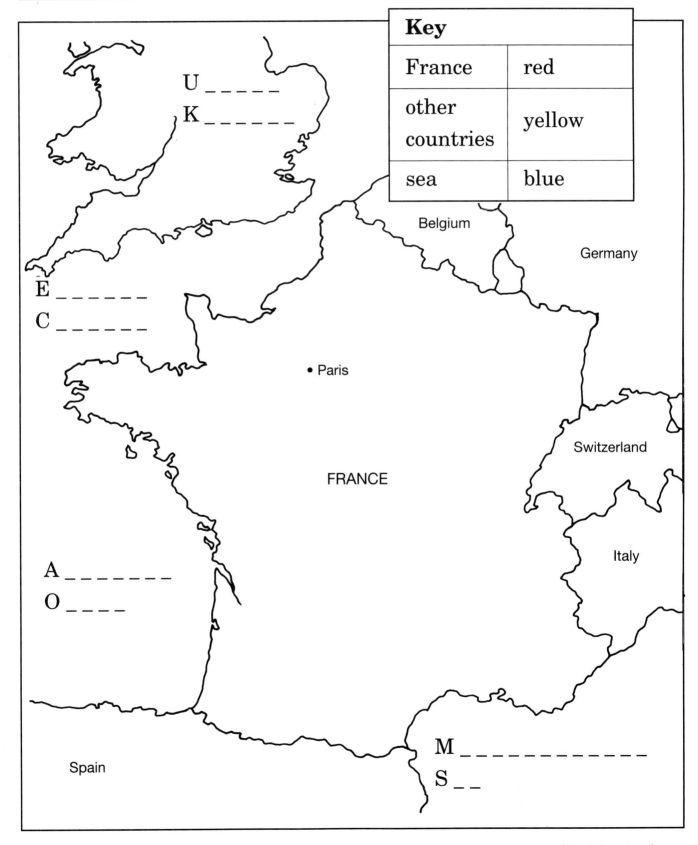

18 France

Name _____

1 Fill in the Fact File for France.

Fact File

Country _____

Capital city _____

Rivers 1 _____

2 _____

Mountains 1 _____

2 _____

Food products 1 _____

2 _____

Industries 1 _____

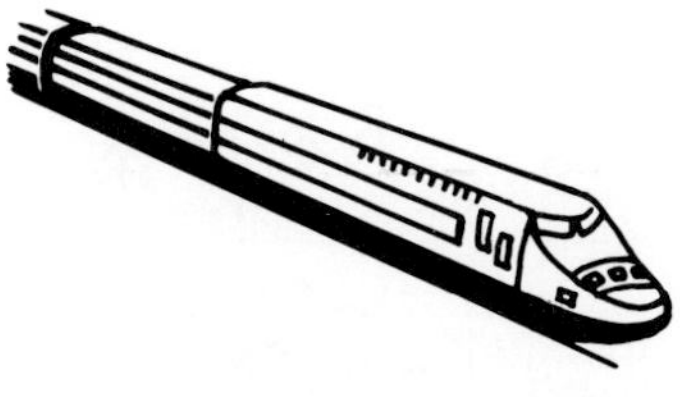

2 _____

 **Asia**   Name _____

1. Colour the symbols in the key.
2. Draw the symbols in the right places on the map. Colour them.
3. Write labels for the things you have shown on the map.

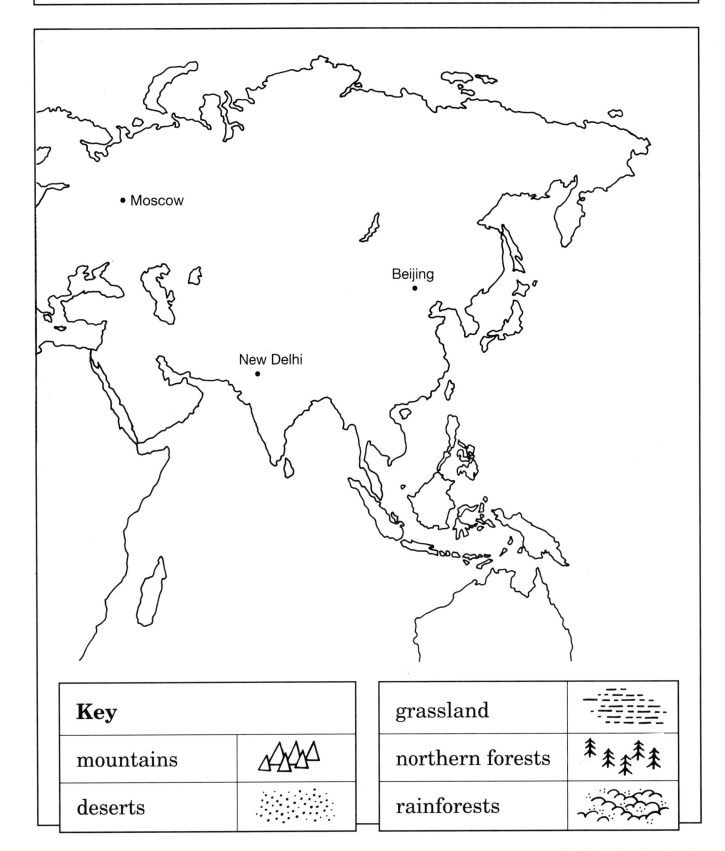

World Watch 1: **World** p57

20 Asia

Name _____

1. Colour the pictures.
2. Name the pictures using this list.
   water tank   baobab tree   school   temple
3. Draw a line from each picture to the right place on the map.

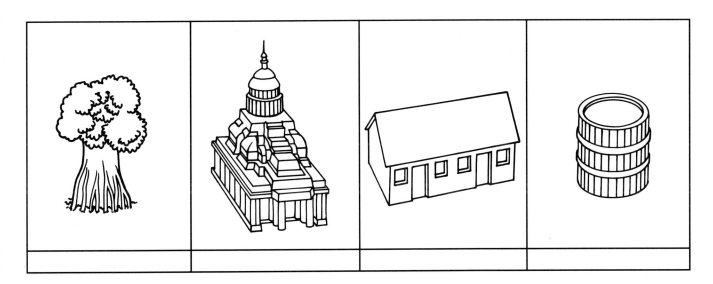

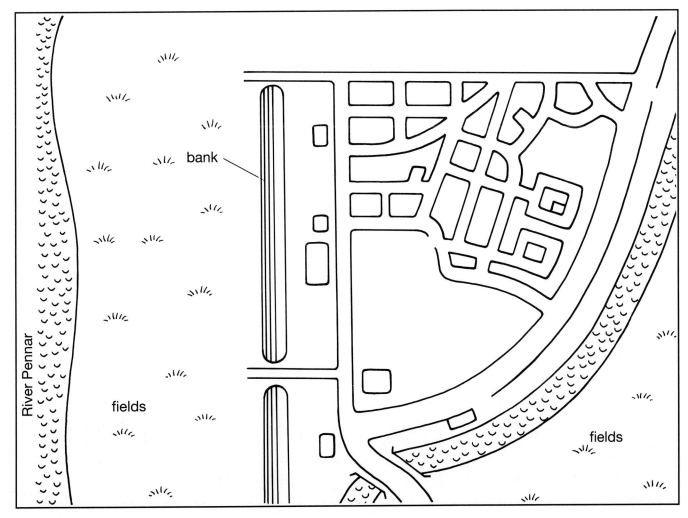

World Watch 1: **World** p60 © Collins Educational 1994

Links to the Scottish Guidelines 5-14

Environmental Studies
Social Subjects: Understanding People and Place

	Contexts and content for development understanding				
	Aspects of the physical and built environment	Ways in which places have affected people and people have used and affected places	Locations, linkages and networks	Making and using maps	

● major focus
○ minor focus

Unit					Main statement
Planet Earth	●			○	natural and physical features of their own locality and how they are used
A Wet Planet		●		○	ways in which weather in different places affects people and nature and ways in which people have learned to adapt to it
Hot and Cold Places		●		○	ways in which weather in different places affects people and nature and ways in which people have learned to adapt to it
A Place to Live	●			○	reasons why settlements differ in character, size, number of people and function
Ways of Travelling			●	○	ways in which people and goods are moved about in their locality
Food and Farming		●		○	ways in which people can affect and change places through their work and leisure
Caring for the Countryside		●		○	reasons why some places are thought to be attractive and valuable and how attraction and value can be enhanced
Scotland	●			○	some major natural and physical features of Scotland
France		●		○	ways in which people can affect and change places through their work and leisure
Asia		●		○	ways in which places affect people's lifestyle

Links to the Northern Ireland curriculum

Unit	Statements of Attainment *	
Planet Earth	Gg1 3h) Gg2 3d) Gg4 2b)	identify major features on globes and maps identify simple features of the physical landscape describe some details of buildings and features they see in their local area
A Wet Planet	Gg1 2a) Gg1 3g) Gg2 3a)	ask questions about human and physical phenomena locate squares on a plan or map using letter/number coordinates recognise that weather is made up of a number of elements
Hot and Cold Places	Gg1 3h) Gg2 2a) Gg2 2b)	identify major features on globes and maps describe ways in which weather influences people's lives recognise that weather in other places differs from that in their own area
A Place to Live	Gg3 3b) Gg3 3c)	recognise that there are different types of dwellings in the local area and elsewhere recognise that people live in different sizes of settlement
Ways of Travelling	Gg1 3c) Gg3 2b) Gg3 3a)	use criteria to sort information obtained from first hand observations explain why people travel identify how some of the goods and services needed in the local community are provided
Food and Farming	Gg1 3a) Gg3 2a)	record and present observations in appropriate written and graphical forms identify some of the goods and services people need
Caring for the Countryside	Gg2 2d) Gg2 3c) Gg5 3)	recognise that plants grow in different materials compare a variety of habitats and their associated plants and animals give reasons for taking up a particular position about a problem
Scotland	Gg1 3f) Gg2 3c) Gg3 3c)	draw simple maps not to scale compare a variety of habitats and their associated plants and animals recognise that people live in different sizes of settlement
France	Gg3 3b) Gg4 3b)	recognise that there are different types of dwellings in the local area and elsewhere identify characteristics of some areas in the wider world which contrast with their home area
Asia	Gg2 2b) Gg4 3b)	recognise that weather in other places differs from that in their own area identify characteristics of some areas in the wider world which contrast with their home area

* These requirements are valid until 1996.

Published by Collins Educational
77-85 Fulham Palace Road, London W6 8JB
An imprint of HarperCollinsPublishers

© Stephen Scoffham, Colin Bridge, Terry Jewson 1994

First published 1994

987654321

ISBN 0 00 315474 2

The authors assert the moral right to be identified as the authors of this work.

All rights reserved. Any educational institute that has purchased one copy of this publication may make duplicate copies of the Copymasters (pages 26-45) for use exclusively within that institution. Permission does not extend to reproduction, storage in a retrieval system, or transmittal, in any form or by any other means, electronic, mechanical, photocopying, recording or otherwise, of duplicate copies for loaning, renting or selling to any other institution without the prior consent in writing of the Publisher.

Printed and bound by Martins the Printers Ltd, Berwick upon Tweed

Design by Chi Leung

Illustrations by Julian Baker